Dedicated to my daughter Destiny

and dancers everywhere

REFLECTIONS OF GRACE

BE A LEADER: MEMORIZE YOUR PART

After my third book, "Moments with Dad" written for my two daughters, I was at a point of complete bliss. My daughters were thrilled with my book, but I felt I needed to do an additional book for my 8-year-old daughter Destiny to show her how much I cherished the time with her as an individual as well. My oldest is 20 and she read "Moments with Dad" in about 6 hours after I gave it to her. She simply said that if I had put so much time and effort to pay a professional photographer, put my daughters on the cover, and spent months writing it directly to my daughters, she needed to read it right away. I cried at the thought that my daughter would feel so touched to get any wisdom from dear old Dad. The book wraps up with seeing my two daughters from two different perspectives. My oldest daughter was just like me and loves psychology and child development while my youngest is still developing today and loves going to ballerina classes. As I sat watching her one day, I started realizing all the lessons that ballet and being a ballerina can teach a person. Both my daughters are leaders in their own special way. They lead not by might and power but by grace and peace. This book will focus on those lessons and more attention to my younger daughter Destiny. I am still learning how to dance in life, but she has taught me simple things. Thank you, Destiny, my little ballerina.

Be A Leader. First, what is a leader? A leader can be good or bad. A leader can take advantage of people. A leader can strive for power and attention. However, the leader I am going to write about is a leader that can lead from the back as well as the front. A true leader always sees their mistakes and wants to improve. In ballet, practice is very important. A ballerina must keep doing a move until they make it look right and be at the right moment in a song or a presentation. A good leader needs to know what she/he stumbles over. The leader then must look around and see who is doing it correctly. This is what life is all about.

When I first started watching my daughter perform ballet, I would follow her eyes. Often, her eyes would be glued to the teacher. However, the teacher would change music or walk around and maybe out of view of the front of the class. Now what should I do? Hesitation and fear would grip my daughter. Do I remember my part? What was the next step? Soon, every little girl is looking at each other and trying to copy the other girls who all seemed lost at this point. The teacher would prance back on the scene and the girls would all breathe a sigh of relief. As this happened time and time again, some girls soon realized they couldn't just depend on the teacher. Then, the teacher would point out that my daughter was out of step because she obviously was watching the girls next to her. Soon, a pattern started to emerge. The more they practiced, the less they relied on the teacher. The more confident they became. Initially, it was quite fun as I watched the heads of the children swivel back and forth trying to see who they should watch. Each child didn't want to be wrong. They didn't want to look like they hadn't paid attention. Like a bunch of penguins, legs flopped here and there, heads bounced around, and arms were making motions like an octopus. I thought I was watching seals swimming.

After a few classes, however, I noticed that about 7 children were regulars and the parents made sure they came every week. It is an inspiration to see fellow Dads taking their daughters to class each week. I imagined only women would be willing to bring their children in pink tutus. Many times, moms did bring their daughters, but on a few occasions, I was indeed proud to not be the only father in the waiting area. I would like to say that you can't make a great leader for civilization or anything, if you are willing to sit on the sidelines as a parent. To the leaders who tirelessly sacrifice for their children, thank you for engaging in the dance.

Out of 7 children in one class, I recognized about 3 wanted to lead. I don't know how this developed or how a person comes to this awakening, but my daughter was one of them. After about the third lesson, she always stood next to the same girl. She was dependent on that one girl to help keep her in line. My daughter had her "dependent" down to one friend to keep her focused and on task. It wasn't that the other ballerinas weren't good or trying. Destiny simply started narrowing the field down to the 2 other leaders. How did she reason these were the good leaders? They didn't need extra attention to straighten up, fly right, or get spoken to by the teacher to address their issues. Eventually, the 3 leaders often hung around each other or made sure they were next to each other. They placed themselves in positions to watch the mirrors and angles. My daughter wanted to get to class early to gain that "positioning". It was like watching chess as they lined up for the class.

I don't want to overlook the other 4. The other 4 children are not less gifted or less inspiring. The other 4 formed their own "group" but they didn't understand positioning as well as the lead 3. It was more like a social club and felt like girls sitting around a play "tea party" at the house. It was fun and something to do but the 4 would continue each time to just "show up", get together with a close friend, and wag their heads each week. When the professional plays and big rehearsals would be given, the 4 would know who to watch and all the eyes would go straight to the 3.

The 3 were independent. They were a bit bossy and loud but not in class. I would watch the 3 as they came out of the class. They were very proud, would be talking about the moves, and then boldly tell their parents, "Let's go", as if now they are in full command of everything. Week after week, I noticed a real focus by the 3 in class. The teacher would start the class and suddenly the 3 had nothing else on their mind or hearts. Focus. Discipline. It was game time and they knew it. The 4 would still be talking a bit and one might think it was a bit of a recess. I would compare the two groups like a football team. You can have a star QB, but if you don't have a good running back or wide receiver, that QB will be sacked a lot. Even if you have a great QB leader, a good running back, and a good wide receiver, you may not win because you don't have the other members of your offensive line blocking for the leaders. In life, we need both groups. Don't let yourself be only in certain groups because as a person, you can't be a leader until you have learned from the back of the pack as well.

My daughter learned from everyone. Yes, as she progressed, she stood next to the other leaders often, but one of the leaders always had a follower next to her. Often, I would see my daughter squeezed between a playful, carefree ballerina and a focused disciplined, "I've waited all week for this" ballerina. We all have been there in life as well. Don't you have a friend that often seemed unfocused and almost seems like the person has very little purpose? The one friend might live one day at a time, enjoying each breath as a blessing. Then, you have a friend who is so driven they make you focus harder and sometimes creates such a passion and drive you can become stressful and angry. We need both types of people in our life. As we developed the other lessons, you will understand how this is very meaningful. Being a leader isn't about boasting and proud behavior but realizing that those care free unfocused people help you while achieving your passions. Some people might say they are goofy, troublesome, and have no principles or ideals. All this may be true.   Take for example a friend who does drugs or drinks too much. You have watched them at their lowest stages of life and shook your head at their misery or choices. However, because you watched them in life, you chose not to be like them. You realized while watching them that they moved the leg the wrong way. Their missed steps allowed you to sense that is not the way the teacher wants you to do the choreography. Soon, you focus more on the teacher and start watching others who are making moves like you. Discipline. Focus. Driven. We can't keep pushing ourselves without also recognizing that those monkeys over there, helped us hone our own skills. Life is a circus and we all know some monkeys in our life. However, even monkeys can teach us things if we are willing to look. A true leader learns from everyone, regardless whether they wear a pink tutu or a black one.

 A true leader learns that everyone can get a movement right now and then. As I mentioned, a true leader learns to lead from the front by leading from the back. If you can't learn from the weakest link in the lowest group, you are not a true leader. A leader is always learning and adapting.

My daughter was turning into a leader. I have seen this development from an early age. The ballet classes helped my daughter's arrogance. She often was too proud and loud at home before ballet classes at age 6. As she learned to watch others, she made mental notes. We never know which group our kids will adopt to more readily.   Don't be disappointed if your child doesn't fit your definition of a leader. The truly great leaders are built by the children who struggle. We all struggle. In some parts of life, we maybe in the monkey group and need to relax more. In some parts of life, we maybe in the leader group. However, everything I will talk about, every ballerina in life, is in the circus.

Leaders are willing to learn from the mistakes of others and the mistakes of themselves. Leaders recognize that improvement comes by loving others where they are at. Leaders, however, also must change positions and locations to become a more professed attribute to others as well maintain discipline and focus. Don't overlook the monkeys of today.   However, they may be helping the leaders of tomorrow and at the same time, a monkey we often overlook will rise to be the greatest leader ever.

One of my favorite disciples in the Bible is Andrew. Many people look at Peter, James, or John as the powerful leaders and speakers. However, as you study the Bible you see Andrew first. Andrew quietly introduces Peter to Jesus and walks away. Again, you see the disciples and Jesus talking about feeding the multitudes and what does Andrew do? He walks up with a little boy with fishes and loaves and walks away quietly. No fanfare. No big part. Andrew was just doing his part. Andrew was a monkey type in the Bible. He isn't a leader. He isn't a flash and dash. We don't know if he got it all right or much about his character. All we see Andrew doing is "his part". Without Andrew, would Peter have preached so boldly? Would so many people have been led to Christ without Andrew doing his one little thing? Certainly not! Then, the "leaders" of the disciples were bogged down in minutia concerning the feeding of the 5000. Here is Andrew doing "his part". Andrew was a monkey in the sense that he may not have had the drive and passion it seemed as a Peter, but he was at least doing something. Peter had to acknowledge Andrew was a vital part to the start of his ministry.   If Peter was a leader, he had to realize that Andrew played a big part of his life as well.

A leader recognizes the importance of "one part". One part could mean a small leg movement or a leap. Every part is a great piece of the bigger movement. A true leader sees the small part that someone plays in their life and slows down long enough to say, "thank you". A leader never ever misses an opportunity to thank the other group for their contribution to their lives.

Maybe you know someone in your life that you don't hang around them often, but they always seem to be there for you, or shows up with a flower, a card, or a snack. This friend may be your Andrew. They know when to show up and do something thoughtful.   Remember to thank them for their part because their part also has become a part of your leadership and abilities.

You may be in a different act of the circus,
 but it wouldn't be a circus without the monkeys.

Take time to be a monkey sometimes.
Leaders learn to relax and not always need to lead.
By not leading, you may become an even better person.

BE HAPPY WITH YOUR PART

Happiness comes from knowing what part you play in a sequence or a play. Many times, there is a real difficulty accepting your child is a monkey lacking real focus at this dance. A parent may believe they have the "star" ballerina. We all want to believe our child will be the standout ballerina and lead even when the practice is continually lackluster. Let me say I am not using the term monkey as a derogatory term, but a fun one. Let me explain.

In a circus, there are trapeze artists, elephants, fire blowers, and a host of other artists. Animals are used less these days in circus acts, but the original "act" was that of a monkey with a magician or a musician on the street corner. In some movies, they show the monkey fleecing the crowd, or distracting from the magician. Some gathered money and some were a shining part of a rather boring act, but the monkey would get the attention and the musician would get money anyway, because of the monkeys. Like in life, monkeys can have lots of talent and fun and laughter. We all need a bit of monkey in us, even if we are a leader. Actually, leaders can't be leaders without a few monkeys swinging all around them. Monkeys all have different talents and can become leaders for short periods of time. I often have considered myself a leader, but in the real sense of the scheme, I am a monkey. I can lead for a bit, but I can't lead long-term nor do I want to. I can't handle the pressure and stress consistently.

I can say my brother is a leader. He handles the tough decisions daily. This does not mean leaders don't have stress, pressure, heartache, pain, or tears. It simply means they appear to have had tougher battles earlier in life and have tougher skin.

The longer you deny whether you are a monkey or a leader the more pain you will have when you finally admit you can't carry the load you thought you could. Parents deal with this let down many ways. We can focus on the fact that the child failed our expectations. Blame the child. We can focus on the fact that we failed the child. Blame the parent. We may even choose to focus on the teacher. Blame the teacher. The real action needed is to look at the practice habits, the number of lessons, or accept the fact that your child may love ballet, but this is not a career or something they are indeed passionate about.

Some of the hardest falls and fails in life whether you are a parent, or a teacher is recognizing that a child is not living up to YOUR expectation. Maybe your child isn't motivated or involved. A lesson during the day would be better suited to your child. Often, however, parents want to live through their kids and fail to see the dreams of their children but instead try to live their own. I have heard parents talk about how they took ballet when they were younger, but they didn't stick with it. Little Suzy is being pressured to perform but she has no passion for dancing, but her mom or dad does.   This failure of expectation is never examined enough by parents, teachers, bosses, or leaders.

Companies often try to fit "A" people into "Z" slots at work. The employee is unhappy and unproductive. They don't function well at night but are placed on night jobs. Even when the employee tells the boss they don't like this position, many times they are kept in that position because that is what the company needs but not what is great for the employee.   However, a happy employee makes for happy atmosphere which normally equates to happy customers who spend money.

This solution is no different with life in general. The reason the world is so miserable is many times we are plugging people into areas not based on talent but by needs and monetary value. Many people of all ages are forced to work for companies and ideals less than humane, but the job pays the bills. Workers tolerate so much hostility because they need live, but they never really are living their passion. Much of life is wasted trying to discover your passion that you are buried emotionally while trying to earn a living.

Now, back to "BE HAPPY WITH YOUR PART". If I am a monkey that keeps dreaming of being a leader, I won't be happy. However, I can be a great monkey. The thing about monkeys are they have so many options of what monkeys to be. You may not be a great piece of the play, but your part of the play may be a key transition to the ending. Your monkey may make the audience laugh simply because they danced left when they should have danced right. They bowed earlier than later with the group. The amazing thing is that this uniqueness makes people smile and laugh. Why?

I have attended several full plays with my daughter at Mendocino College Theater. As I sat thru others many audience members would remember the cute mistakes of the younger children. They would remember the lady bug that slipped while the one behind picked her up. As I heard this in the hallways, I noticed that we could relate to being a monkey. People needed to laugh because we all have been monkeys…. even the leaders we look up to, have been monkeys.

We have lost our drive and passions in life because things happen. We believe we can control the whole Nutcracker play perfectly, yet suddenly some tights were ripped, a shoe is missing, and the lights are flashing wrong. We scramble to put things back together. Suddenly, a person we don't expect to be a leader strolls out with a shoe, a pair of tights, and an extension cord for the bad wiring. This is Monkey Joe. I trust him to give a presentation or put a play together. I wouldn't trust him to do much for me, but there is the monkey. Talented in the area I need now and answering the call. They swing in to lighten the mood and relieve stress both to the leaders and the other monkeys. We all laugh at the monkeys but often we don't remember the leaders. We expected the leaders to lead. We take the leaders for granted. When a leader becomes a monkey, we feel they let us down. If a Pastor or a teacher acts foolish or goofy, we don't expect it, so we tend to be like a parent who puts all the expectations on the child. Thus, the leader is expected to be a leader without any real accolades but when they lose the grip on leadership and need a fun moment, they failed to lead to the people around them. Monkeys have the lower expectations, so they can choose passions over leadership. However, when they step up and save the day or can lead for short moments, they not only receive praise and notoriety, people start hanging out with the monkeys more. The monkeys may have a upside and potential. However, the downside is that they often are not passionate enough to lead overall in many avenues. The monkeys show up to save the day, make us laugh, and enjoy the simplicity of the moments. Leaders, however, can drive us to new heights and goals. Leaders can bring passion, success, drive, commitment, but also unresolved hurt, pressure, and stress. Monkeys tend to be less stressed about things in life because they know to live in the moment. Monkeys can get into trouble by "living in the moment" too much. Leaders often think long term. Don't get me started on whether I think Washington DC has more monkeys or leaders, I need to finish this book and I have other goals in my life planned.

In order to be happy with your part, you need to know in your heart, whether you tend to be more monkey or leader. Remember, a monkey can become a leader by saving the day or leading for short periods of time at what they are passionate about. However, they are more fun loving, less driven, and seem to acknowledge their limitations in areas. I have found monkeys to be more honest with themselves and often more honest with others. Leaders on the other hand are often focus driven, not people driven. The goals they have will be reached by doing whatever is necessary to get it right. More practice. More time. More screaming at the monkeys who flop all over the stage. Yet the leader is learning from the monkeys. "Hey monkey, you didn't bend right." The monkey just smiles and says, "Show me how then". The leader gets tense. Did she do it right last time? How many people are watching me? Is the teacher watching me do this as well? The pressure is on. The curtain is drawn up. Did she remember her cues? Did she remember her part or was she so concerned with the monkey? As she continues dancing flawlessly, the monkey now gets it right and the show looks perfect until another monkey slipped on the banana peel. How did that get there?

And the audience laughs and smiles.

The monkeys are always devising ways to lighten the mood.
Are you a monkey or a leader?   Be happy with your part.
You might find a banana peel somewhere on the stage of your life.
Remember to laugh. I am a monkey. Proud of it.

KNOW THE STORY

If you know your part, whether it be a leader or a monkey, you can then have a purpose. This purpose is to help others. Leaders help the monkeys maintain a sense of direction. After all, a leader is more focused but needs to laugh. However, we all look up to leaders to know what the greater purpose is and how one part is important in the grand scheme of things. Unfortunately, even though leaders help the monkeys, they too often forget to just do their part and instead they bark at the monkeys. Soon, a leader is in the middle of their part and stops to yell at a monkey. This set of events happens way too often in life.

Imagine the play is a play of Cinderella. The leader is Cinderella with grace and flair. The audience is mesmerized by her beauty and attention to detail. Yet here are the monkeys, the wicked step sisters who can't get it right. The good news is even if the wicked step sisters mess up, many will perceive it to be part of the play and focus back on the main ballerina, Cinderella. Suddenly, the leader playing Cinderella focuses so much on the bumbling and blundering of the other players in the script and the banana peels laying all over the stage, she forgot something. She forgot to even put on her glass slippers. The Prince dances her around, the clock strikes midnight, and as she runs off the stage, she remembers she is to leave a glass slipper behind. However, she never put them on to begin with. She frantically runs off the stage, grabs the slipper and runs back on stage to "drop it". The audience now sees the leader as flawed and perhaps she isn't as good as we thought. Not only does she second guess herself, the audience knows this wasn't part of the play, and even more, the main teacher wonders if the leader is capable of the pressure. The leader will now beat herself up and try to focus more until that banana peel gets back in the way. There simply is no "relaxing" when it comes to being a leader. Either a leader gets it all right and finds fault with the monkeys or she spends too much time on the monkeys and fails miserably herself and she cries inside because now she is a monkey herself...or feels like one.

Once you know your part, you need to understand the story or vision of the entire scene. One cannot be engaged in "Hamlet" movements while actually being in the "Nutcracker". Monkeys need to notice the leader and the stress she or he has.

Likewise, leaders need to notice when the monkeys are so out of line and character that she needs to lead more. In parenting, we might call this discipline. Your child is acting like a monkey way too often. Your monkey doesn't have passion for ballet but sometimes monkeys can have no passion for people either. They won't help, they won't see the big picture. One might say they are on drugs or hallucinations.

Yet the leaders need the monkeys because leaders can fail at the big picture. Leaders can look at the task and never look at people either.

In business, the director of operations has many tasks at hand. She instructs the monkeys on deadlines, opportunities, character, decorum, and much more. However, the monkeys don't have the same drive as the director of operations. Monkeys do not receive the same benefits of wealth, opportunity, appreciation, or education that a leader has developed through their "drive to succeed". Monkeys are often put down and trampled under the passion and drives of others. The morale is often flexible and changing, sometimes daily. A leader has passion, but monkeys do too. Monkeys, however, have a different vision of how things should operate. Leaders do not like monkeys, but they need monkeys. Monkeys often may not like leaders, but they know they need leaders. Whereas a leader may make much more money, options, can set their schedules sometimes, and not do manual labor, a monkey makes less money has more stress on other levels of measuring up, and know they will rarely be a leader. Monkeys have a difficult time realizing both potential and recognizing they will not be a strong leader. Leaders have a difficult time focusing the monkeys and bearing the burden that even their best efforts may not be enough. Leaders can often be depressed so they push harder and harder, until they slip on the banana peel of life and feel they failed somewhere or someone. I'd rather be a monkey.

Let me put this another way. You are in the 60's or 70's. You are either a hippie or a government backer. A hippie might just jump in a car and go where ever their heart desired. Some VW van pulls up and invites you in. No cares, the monkeys are carefree, but their needs are met. They live by the seat of their pants openly talking to everyone and everything. They can sit quietly and do absolutely nothing.

They can and have done drugs, traveled the world, and sat in a hot tub without clothing. Now, here comes the leader. The leader walks up and wonders why you haven't joined the military, or why are you not protesting. The leader may or may not have traveled the world. The leader hasn't traveled the world necessarily but if they did it was for business, not pleasure. The leader is reserved because in business you can't have a weak side. You can't open yourself up to the monkeys because a weakness may topple the company or plan. The idea is to get the play's idea across. The leader is focused so much on the overall big picture, they will miss a detail or two.

One day, the leader slips and needs to focus. The leader must think about where he or she messed up. "Did that person make me slip? Did I say something wrong? Did a monkey get out of line? Was the timing wrong?" As the leader continues to ponder all the negative ramifications of what went wrong with the grand business meeting, he takes a breather and decides to go to the local spa with hot tubs. The leader is worried about a great many things. He planned everything so well. He knew and practiced the presentation. He had all the reports and surveys done by the monkeys. Where was the mistake? What monkey can I blame? As the leader climbs in the hot tub, he sees a friend from work, a person he considers a "monkey" who can't get their act together. "Oh great. I can't even relax here because the monkey may see my frustration. I need to be on my best behavior" the leader ponders.

Soon, he notices the monkey is without clothes. "The emperor has no clothes" the leader thinks to himself. The leader smiles and laughs. The monkey is smiling but silent. The leader mentions work, stress, life, and his future plans. The monkey smiles and seems to be fighting a good belly laugh. The leader is growing angry. The leader is now mad that the monkey is laughing at him and his life. The monkey senses the stress and begins to leave. As the monkey wraps a towel around his waist, the monkey simply says, "Enjoy your day. It is a great place to relax right now. Nice talking with you".

The leader wonders what just happened. Did he say something wrong? Was this the monkey that messed up at the office? Should I talk to the monkey about being nude? Should I fire this monkey? Suddenly, the monkey employee is scrutinized for every action and response. Finally, the care taker of the spa tells the leader it is time to get out and looks at him with a look of disdain and perplexity. "What are you looking at? I am a customer and you can't treat me like this" he blurts out with frustration.

"I am sorry sir, but you can't be in the hot tub with your business suit on. I was just thinking that a person like yourself has too much on his mind and appears overworked. You need to relax right now. Enjoy your day. Stay a little longer but please remove your clothes and change into a swimsuit. Yes, the emperor has no clothes.

The leader thinks back to what the monkey had said. He realized he too was overworked and not stopping to realize that although he thought the monkey was out of line, out of character, out of touch with reality, and laughing at him, he really was not the foolish one. The leader just slipped on another banana peel.
The leader had become a monkey. Just as the monkey can become a leader in these moments. Relax. In the grand scheme of the play, you are simply another monkey. The play will go on. The audience will laugh. The curtain will drop, and the audience will leave. Remember to take a moment to bow....

Even if you forgot your clothes or are wearing a suit,
        Or failed to remember to bring those glass slippers.

Laugh at yourself and life. You will slip on banana peels. You will be in a suit while the monkeys try to laugh. Monkeys are the heart of the show. They will smile and laugh but rarely are so judgmental. They don't have a plan other than to meet people and live within their means.

Monkeys really do have the KEY to the story and your life. When you respect and love your monkeys, you will have fun more, relax more, and the monkeys will teach you how to lead by seeing the tropical insights of people's lives.

Now, get out of your business suit and grab a robe. Don't forget the banana peel because we are going to slip into something more comfortable and laugh.

The leader exits the hot tub in his suit and the high heeled glass slippers.

It is midnight, and the leader hangs his head. The leader thought he knew the purpose of the play.   The leader thought he had it all together. The leader was condemning. The monkey was accepting.

Know the Story: Love, Laugh, Live

LAUGH AT YOUR MISTAKES

Love. Laugh. Live. Simple. However, we often fail to love our own mistakes. This statement is totally true for an absolute leader who fails to realize they "too" started out as a monkey trying to figure out what truly motivates and drives them. Love yourself in the moments of confusion. Laugh at your mistakes. Live the moment.

As I commented in the last chapter, leaders have a dynamic problem. In their quest for a goal or perfect play, a ballerina will glare at the less than passionate monkeys. The leader's focus is always drifting from memorizing their own activities to the activities of others. Imagine the judge in a tennis match. They watch the ball side to side, moving their head with the movement of the ball. Their attention is pure focus but really the focus can only be on the ball, not the players. A ball called "out" incorrectly suddenly could cost a player the game. The judge doesn't have time to listen to people in the audience or even glance into the sky to watch a bird. One mistake and the game will change. Everything relies on the calling of the game accurately.   This type of focus can't be taught. It is a passion for the game. It is a passion we all have, when we find out what we are passionate about!

A leader in ballet trains and trains and trains. Every movement needs to be absolutely perfect. Perhaps the leader believes that everyone will applaud and remember her efforts. Perhaps the leader doesn't want to be known as a monkey slipping all over the stage.   Perhaps though the leader simply loves what she does. If she could only make the play itself stand out! Oh no, here comes those less than enthusiastic monkeys. Now, the leader needs to not only perfect her part, but now she must try to keep the monkeys motivated enough to follow through, even if only for the actual play. Like a ping pong ball on a table, she dances gracefully trying to remember her part, and keeping an eye on the monkeys. She motivates and teaches. She inspires and addresses others with grace or with conflict. However, the leader only gets satisfaction from knowing the play went well. The leader will always critique her own performance and remember where the monkey waited too long to follow another monkey or even ran into her during the performance. A true leader is always trying to improve. Improvement is the key to discovering the joy in what you do have a passion to do. Nonetheless, the leader fights the depression and angst of never measuring up. She despises the monkeys because things aren't going as expected. It is always someone's fault because the expectation is so high. A goal driven passionate person will always want more, dream more, achieve more, and even "contemplate" more. A dreamer will think of the many multiple missed opportunities, the ways to improve the performance, and the monkey that stopped to look at the ladybug on the stage. A dreamer rarely stops to see the moment. The failed attempts of a leader push them to achieve more. A dreamer or leader will battle the expectations vs the reality of a situation. It is a conflict within them that can't be resolved. Dreamers most likely were told that they "couldn't do it" or "wasn't good enough". For whatever reason, a leader may push themselves to prove to others that they can do it whether the person has a passion for it or not.

Proving "worth" as a leader to others or themselves becomes a passion. This is what truly separates the monkeys from the dreams. Motivation.

Motivation is a multi-dimensional monster. Motivation can be for others like parents, teachers, pastors, and spouses as well. Motivation can be simply because you absolutely love ballet, sports, math, helping others, and much more. Motivation can be an inner spirit that makes you feel the joy of youth and life. Few, however, find this motivation.   Many times, the motivation unfortunately is money or fame. Money motivation puts a dollar value on your worth. Companies and others place a dollar value on your time and energy resources to such a degree that you believe your innate value is $14.35 an hour. Bills must be paid, food bought, kids schooled, and in the quest to be responsible, we settle for less than our best passions.   Society has us sell our dreams for the sake of providing a home, a life, and doing our duty. There is nothing wrong with being a loving, caring parent or provider but eventually you will find that something like simply being a robot for others won't make you happy. You lost your passion. You need to find it and that may mean not looking at the money.

I have worked at Safeway for 20 years. 5 years before at Walmart. Most of my life I have worked in the retail business sector. I could lead for periods of time and do great work. I consider myself quite an organizer, but I have also had 3 breakdowns in 15 years. As I walked out crying after my 3rd mental breakdown, I felt "empty". Alone. I had spent my entire life "planned". I planned what basic furniture I would have when I moved out at age 13. By age 15, I bought my first couch and tucked it away in my bedroom removing the bed. Step by step I planned my life to be a good husband, a dependable person, and a loving father. I attended college and received my associate degree in Accounting. After one year sitting behind a desk, I realized I had become an Accountant not because I wanted to, but because I was trying to show my Dad I was good in math and could do it. Wrong motivation. Four years after graduation, I was working at Walmart, but it seemed to fast-paced. I had my first daughter and my sense of duty and purpose was even more pressing. I started working at Safeway in 1998 and within 12 years, I had my second child. Duty and responsibility gripped me. Four years after my second child, I slipped on the banana peel again and ended back in the mental hospital this time voluntarily. Finally, 4 years later after the last incident, here I was in my car, crying profusely and shaking hysterically. I was lying to myself. I was a monkey who could lead for short periods of time, but none of these things were my passion. I hadn't discovered my passion but kept trying to lead in areas because my family needed me too. We needed the money and my motivation stemmed from their needs, not my own.

As I sat there shaking and crying, I felt the sense, "I AM DONE". I had lied for the last time about the limits I had, the motivation I had, the planning game, and the expectations of others. I barely could drive home 15 miles away. Looking back, I should have seen a clear sign. The very first song I heard in Safeway was Soul Asylum's "RUNAWAY TRAIN". It is a song meant for runaway children or lost children in society. Ironically, they still play it 20 years later. As I remembered that first song as I walked in, I couldn't imagine walking back into the store to work, ever again. It didn't matter the position, the noise, the pay, or the benefits. It didn't matter who I had to say "no" to. It didn't matter the expectations. It didn't matter any longer. I had lost myself in the need to fulfill others. I had managed to lie to myself most of my life under the sense of duty to others, sacrifice, and principles. These virtues are all noble and should always be looked upon with respect and honor. Veterans, police officers, fire fighters, and first responders all fit the criteria of sacrifice and duty. Most of the time, however, they are passionate about what they do, helping others. I had to stop the illusion that I was a leader. I was a monkey trying to lead but kept falling and failing.

As a leader of my family, I spent my life trying to plan, organize, and improve the lives of others. Now, I was a broken piece of glass lying on the floor. I didn't fit the lifestyle of a retail person. I had organizational skills but lacked clarity on other things. My mind had simply become events and duties. I didn't enjoy what I was doing, and I am sure I wasn't enjoying life. My passion was gone. My motivation betrayed me. It was raining that night and cold. It was perfect. It was me. I loved overcast clouds. I loved the beach. I loved sunsets and sunrises. I loved helping people. Yet something was wrong. I did everything by the book. Married. Kids. Job. Bill paying. Attend church. Pray.

Broken. I wasn't laughing anymore. I was crying. I couldn't love anymore because I didn't love my job. I didn't love others because I didn't love myself. I was lying to myself to make others happy. I had sacrificed my life and myself too much and walked away. I don't know when I first laughed after that, because I was rocked to my core. There is nothing funny when you look at yourself and realize you have nothing left to give others. I do know when I did find myself again. It was a simple place and a simple time. A memory.

When my mom and I first came to Ukiah, she knew her two sons were depressed from a divorce, a sudden move, and new people. Our world had crashed. I am pretty sure we weren't laughing then either. She had very little money but drove us over to Navarro beach. I drove there a few days after I was crying in the car. Again, I smiled. Something called me there. Something I needed. I needed the ocean, not simply occasionally. Daily. I walked up and down the beach thinking of my mom, choices she had to make, and the difficulty we endured together. She has had Alzheimer's for 4 years now and you might believe the beach would make me sad. It didn't. It made me smile. It brought "me" to the forefront. "What would you like to do today" she would ask. Mom never asked a one-dimensional question. Her question implied the present as well as the future.

Mom often took us to the coast to relieve stress. It was home. Ukiah was never my home. I simply had stopped short of realizing my dream. In my life I had settled early for something I needed. I had slipped on a banana peel more than once and failed to realize I needed to get up and finish the performance.

I love the place in my life right now. Simply because I don't know what is next. I know what I want. I know where I want to live. I only laugh now because it took me this long to realize it was so close and yet so far. I must risk it all to find the peace I have only enjoyed a few times in my life. Every sense of duty and sacrifice is gone and exchanged for motivation for me. The passion of my life. Is it a place or a purpose? I am unsure.

With 3 mental breakdowns, I now see my slips and falls. I spent so much time and energy on watching the monkeys, I kept slipping and failing on my part in the play. I love the outdoors. I love writing. I want to help others see their passions and dreams. I want to help the mentally ill and counsel the helpless. My passion for the mentally ill and others came from slipping on my own banana peels.

As I watched the other monkeys in my life who looked up to me as a leader, I slipped and slipped. I scolded the monkeys. I couldn't see my own slips. Those banana peels were mine, because I was a monkey too. I was a monkey trying to be helpful and lead others in fields that was not my calling or desire. When I started to see my own life history, I saw the gooey mess on the stage.

In the past few weeks, I see a cherry on top of the banana split.

The stage is a mess. Banana peels are everywhere. The music is still playing.

Grab me a spoon. Let's eat. Too much dessert for me to eat alone.

Banana Splits are meant to be devoured and not stared at.

Bon Appetit'

SOMEBODY'S WATCHING YOU

We have looked at the seemingly unmotivated monkeys. The monkeys seem to not be as focused or passionate about ballet or the task at hand. It isn't because they aren't motivated, it is because this is not their calling or favorite thing to do. On some things or at some moments, they can really be focused, but the teacher notices the difference between the monkeys and the leaders.

We have looked at the leaders. The leader is not the teacher. The leader of the ballerinas is the most focused. She watches the monkeys and watches herself and perfects her movements. Life is a plan, and everything must be in perfect sequence and step. The monkeys watch the leader when they feel the need to but not all the time. The monkeys are having too much fun and the leader is frustrated. The leader is often even frustrated with her own missteps and when expectation didn't meet reality, the leader is quite disappointed but picks herself back up and tries to create a perfect sequence of events, even if she needs to go shake some monkeys from the tree. The leaders watch the monkeys. The monkeys watch what they want to, who they want to, and when they want to.

Then, there are the squirrels. Squirrels are well grounded, so to speak. You will never understand the whole scene until you understand the conversation of squirrels. I learned this simply sitting quietly in the lobby waiting for my daughter to finish ballet class.

Squirrels are the groundwork crew of the monkeys but are leaders as well. Squirrels also believe they have it all together. They have gone through the dance of life but keep believing they are leaders and not monkeys. Parents. Parents deal with nuts all day long. They roll them around. They tuck them away. They throw them at monkeys. They are forced into being leaders simply because they have seen a few acorns on the ground and in the trees. Parents scamper here and there trying to corral the monkeys. The monkeys are the majority of the ballet class. The two or three leaders or stand-outs of the class usually stay behind in class perfecting their routine, so the play goes well. They are the now free to focus without the monkeys, as the monkeys run out to the parents. The squirrels now must lead once again and start moving. Parents understand and laugh at the thought that their kids are monkeys. We see them act like monkeys, swing all over the place, smash dishes, destroy living rooms, and move all over. Where are they? What do you think you are doing? The only thing that can keep the monkey in line is a squirrel. A squirrel simply is "NUTS" and doesn't know it. A squirrel has learned the dance between leading and being a monkey on the flip of a switch. Most squirrels are monkeys that learned to be leaders. The parent may lead a fast-paced rigorous schedule. The parent shuffles the child monkey to this sports program, to ballet, and home. Life is moving so fast; the squirrel can't decide if it is time to climb the tree or grab a nut. A monkey may never EVER be a leader. A monkey can sit all his life and just float through life without a true purpose. We often say they "haven't grown up" or "found their purpose in life". A "hippie" monkey may never really take a lead at anything in life and doesn't care what you think of him. A "trans-monkey" has learned a bit what it takes to lead at important times and be helpful to the leader. A "trans-monkey" adds a bit to the performance but never wants the true lead for any length of time. Squirrels are made from "trans-monkeys". Squirrels are duty bound and always stocking up for winter. They are often high energy planners, but don't realize- THEY ARE STILL MONKEYS pretending to be squirrels.

Why are parents Squirrel Monkeys? I often would sit and listen to parents in the lobby. Some were watching their kids in ballet. They couldn't hear the instruction of the teacher or see the whole picture. They would laugh, and critique both the leaders and the monkeys. Others would be planning their day like a military general down to the last second or talk about how the day went terribly wrong. Some of the squirrels would share their stories of nutty behaviors or roll a nutcase story over to another squirrel as a sign of friendship. As for me, I was the monkey watching the squirrels. I am a Squirrel Monkey. I am in my 40's and I see nuts all the time. I think I saw one in the mirror today, but my vision was blurry, so I will have to check the mirror a few times to see which one I am.

Nuts. Nuts to a squirrel is the little monkeys and their stories. We can't believe they are having fun. We have things to do. We need to get ready for winter. We need to jump on that branch and swing, but the monkey is taking up too much room and time. What we didn't notice, the little monkeys were still teaching the squirrels about life. The little monkeys were knocking the nuts out of the tree, down to our level on the ground. The squirrels are always on the ground looking up at a tree full of monkeys and wondering why they can't get their act together. The monkeys are having fun. The squirrels grew up, but they never try to climb up to the monkey's level.

Squirrel monkeys often do the same thing as leaders even when they are bigger, stronger, more educated. They argue in the lobby about things. They argue about how life is going. They argue about who is worthier and who has done more work. Yet sometimes, yes sometimes, the parents in the lobby would laugh and cry watching the circus of life and the swinging of monkeys in the class. Across the squirrel's face would be smiles. We remember being crazy. We remember simple things and simple moments. Then, we remember the moment we dropped our own banana peels and nuts. The squirrels love the art of sharing. Squirrels understand that sharing is the key to the ballet class. Sharing information. Sharing love. Sharing stories. Sharing the gift of each other.

As the Squirrel Monkeys gather the nuts of their lives, they realize they are picking up valuable pieces of their own dance of life. In the end, the squirrel monkeys will understand it wasn't about being a monkey or being a leader monkey. It was about sharing your monkey business with others. You maybe gathering walnuts, or peanuts, or hazelnuts but guess what squirrels? You were a monkey to begin with and you will be a monkey in the end.

The more you see monkeys in your life, remember you were one. You thought you were looking down on those crazy monkeys. No, you should have been looking up to the monkeys. You are a squirrel on the ground with nuts on the ground around you. The nuts are the stories people tell you about their life. The nuts make the squirrels happy.

We have a little bit of time left in class. Pick the nuts on the ground around you and start eating.

Better yet, go climb the tree. The trees have a few nuts still hanging.

If the monkeys don't get in the way, you might get hear their story.

Now, go look in the mirror again.

We are all "NUTS" aren't we.

Some people just have more Nutty stories than others.

Walnuts anyone?

THE GRACEFUL PROS

This chapter is dedicated to Piper, the ballet teacher who greatly inspired by daughter; also, Ron Ford, an English teacher who inspired me to write.

What is a Pro? A Pro is a teacher or a leader. A leader may become a teacher but that doesn't make them a PRO. There are many people who strive to be at the top or at the very least, the top of their game but that doesn't mean they enjoy being the teacher or enjoy dealing with the monkeys or the other leaders. Let's make a separation between the two main groups: The basic monkey has a free-flowing spirit. The leaders try their hardest to keep the monkeys in some sense of purpose and order but are never happy with themselves. They strive for some unreal expectation for themselves, the monkeys, and the play themselves. They are extreme critics but have very little fun or satisfaction for what they are doing. Let's call the leaders, Chipmunks. Chipmunks run around with nuts in their cheeks all the time with a very much erratic behavior of purpose and goals. However, if you want a task done, ask a chipmunk.

A Pro, however, is often a leader who has started to enjoy the journey. A pro knows that the monkeys are necessary in the life of the play. A pro also knows the leaders can help elevate the play to new heights. However, it is a balance between order and grace. Grace must be given to the monkeys whose hearts are not quite into the ideal. The Pro smiles at the craziness of the monkeys because the Pro sees parts of the character of monkey. Thus, a ballet teacher creates choreography and steps and routines. All the while, it is the monkeys' attitude that makes the teacher so special. However, it is the discipline of the leader that makes her fight for success and drives her passion. A balance must be maintained.

A true teacher is a great leader not because of the art of perfectionism or drive. It is the passion of **loving exactly every moment of the dance**. Professionals in life love to PROFESS. Profess means they love what they do and love talking about it. They wake up with a smile looking forward to each day, each activity, each moment spent with the monkeys and the chipmunks. At the end of the day, they found the balance between Joy and Routine.   Therefore, I am going to call the teacher/pros "**RACCOONS**".

Raccoons have many gifts and they can mask their characters well at any given point. They can laugh with the monkeys in the group, knowing they have been goofy in life as well. They can push themselves onward and upward with drive and determination like the Chipmunks. They can go sit in the lobby and chat it up with the squirrels, sharing wonderful nutty stories of all those monkeys and chipmunks.   Raccoons can climb the tree or stay on the ground. Professionals have many different masks and can change them so smoothly and frequently you don't know what they will say or do!

The true talent of the Professional is that they can inspire both monkeys and chipmunks. Not all chipmunks however love what they do. You can have a career or a job that makes you push and achieve but that doesn't make you love what you do.   Many people wake up, go to work, and achieve great success but they do it for family, for esteem, for fame, for money, but not necessarily for themselves or their own happiness and worth. I should know, I have been there.

Growing up I wanted to study animals, particularly Marine Biology. I had a passion for working with seals and dolphins and marine life. I believe this passion started with attending Monterey Bay Aquarium. The "dream" was to study and learn the art of life at sea. Then, life hit.   My parents divorced, and the finances weren't very good. I took a job to help my single mom. Soon, college slipped away. I ended up working retail for a few years and finally went to a trade school to get my accounting degree. I figured I was good at math and the degree was "notoriety". I would officially "be someone".   I received my associate degree and worked in an office for one year, but it wasn't me. I wasn't happy with very little interaction. I would dream numbers and accounts. After a year, I went back to

Chipmunk took the walnuts quickly to Mr. and Mrs. Squirrels house. As the seasoned squirrels answered the door, Chipmunk replied,

"Here are the walnuts Raccoon promised. I slipped on a banana peel on the way over. Those darn monkeys get in the way! Sorry, but I need to hurry, I am running out of time to get my supplies before winter. I haven't gathered hardly any acorns at all for winter. If I don't make it to next spring, you will know I gave you the walnuts as Raccoon asked." Chipmunk replied, out of breath.

Just then Mrs. Squirrel, sneaks up behind Mr. Squirrel.
"Give him some of these banana peels that slipped in our hole. Raccoon could use these as well." Mr. Squirrel must have seen the look on chipmunk's face.

"Banana Peels?" Chipmunk said startled.

Mr. Squirrel smiled with a benevolent grin.

"Hurry along, Mr. Chipmunk. Lots of work to do. Raccoon needs the banana peels really bad!" Mr. Squirrel chuckled.

Chipmunk was puzzled, "I didn't know Raccoon collected banana peels. Why did Raccoon also have acorns in her paws?" Chipmunk thought to himself.

Chipmunk was very confused. Chipmunk didn't want to see any more banana peels. He knew he was wasting valuable time. It was becoming cold and damp. In Mr. Chipmunk's hands were several banana peels. Up out of the hole, Chipmunk crawled. Where was Raccoon now?

Only one monkey remained now. The bananas were gone. The squirrels were comfy in their hole.

"Everyone is ready for winter but me" stumped Mr. Chipmunk.

Mr. Chipmunk looked at the banana peel one more time. Suddenly, the last monkey threw one last banana peel that hit Chipmunk squarely on the head. Chipmunk scurried up the tree to his home in the tree. Finally, Chipmunk was going to give a monkey a piece of his mind.

"Monkeys treat me like trash" he angrily thought.

The monkey quickly swung away on tree limbs and out of sight.

As Chipmunk sat on the branch near his home, he saw something move. It was Raccoon.

"What was Raccoon doing up here? What is going on? Everyone is thinking about themselves! I am going to starve, and everyone wants me to help them. What about me? Chipmunk was shouted furiously.

Chipmunk wandered over to Raccoon in the tree.

"All done. Chipmunk. Thanks for your help!" Raccoon replied with a grin.

"Help! All I ever do is help! I try to get things done and I get banana peels thrown directly at me. I carried the walnuts to the squirrels who have enough food now. Even Mrs. Squirrel gave me banana peels to feed you! This is crazy. I am tired of helping everyone! I am going to starve. The monkeys are crazy. The squirrels are too slow to do their job and I haven't figure out what you do. I never see you in action. I see you give a lot of direction but never work. Maybe that is why you have a mask on. You are the thief. You are a bandit taking advantage of everyone! Is that it? Tell me. I'm tired of being used!"

Raccoon laughed. "Oh Chipmunk! Did you see your home? You are all packed for winter."

Chipmunk ran over to his hole in the tree and saw his home littered with acorns. In other holes were acorns as well. Even some monkey fur was nestled for a warm bed in the home. Chipmunk was puzzled.

"Raccoon. What am I missing? How did the acorns get in there? I didn't gather any. I have been keeping all my efforts in my chubby cheeks because I figured I wouldn't get to eat much during the winter. Every time I stuffed my cheeks, those monkeys threw a banana peel at me and I would slip and fall, the acorns would fly out of my mouth and I would start again. I even slid into the tree one time and blacked out. It seemed I was moving so fast, but I didn't get anything done", Chipmunk said with a confused look on his face.

Raccoon could hardly stop laughing.

"Chipmunk, the monkeys were throwing you the banana peels to help you work faster. I eat the banana peels and store them for winter. The banana peels help you focus more and slide them to the tree. As you often black out or lose focus, I run up and down the tree to save you time. I have been putting acorns in your holes all year. The monkeys added some bedding to help you sleep comfortably after all those slips and falls. We hoped you would learn to use them like surfboards. Nevertheless, we all get a good laugh from your slides. It reminds us that we are all monkeys at times. You didn't see me because I try not to be seen. I don't need the credit. I just like to help people."

Chipmunk smiled. "You mean to tell me that the monkeys are helping me move faster to my goal? You use the banana peels that I slide to the tree? You help Mr. and Mrs. Squirrel with their nuts as well? However, you all laugh at me?"

"Yes. The monkeys throw the banana peels, usually in front of you. You slide over to the tree or sometimes hit the tree. The banana peels are waiting for me to gather after I come down from putting acorns in your home. Mr. and Mrs. Squirrel are too old to gather the nuts fast or climb the tree. The wild monkeys try to knock nuts down to the ground but sometimes they don't quite have enough. My part is to help make sure everyone has what they need. If you didn't make that crazy sound surfing on banana peels, we wouldn't laugh. The look on your face and the sounds you make, encourage the monkeys to shake the tree with laughter and nuts fly to the ground more often for Mr. and Mrs. Squirrel and helps me to gather more as I go up the tree. By slipping and sliding on the banana peels, we laugh at your "surfing" which encourages all of us. You play a critical role. Without your surfing, the squirrel family dies, monkeys would simply be hitting you with bananas too far from the tree, and I would go hungry as well. We need you chipmunk. We all play a part. Hurry along Chipmunk. A warm winter's nap awaits, and I must get these banana peels back to my log. Thank you, Mr. Chipmunk. The Valley wouldn't be as wonderful without you." Raccoon begins to walk away with rainbow on the horizon.

"I am useful then?" Chipmunk asked.

"Yes. If you weren't here, the monkeys wouldn't laugh. If the monkeys don't laugh, we don't have our nutty stories to tell and share about how fast you are moving, and many people wouldn't get fed for the winter. Thanks for the banana peels my friend"

"Have to leave now" she says as Raccoon wanders away.

The monkeys were all gone, a few nuts remained, and the first drops of rain splattered on Mr. Chipmunk's nose. Chipmunk scurried to his den and into his warm bed, content that he too was making a difference.

Next spring arrived, and Chipmunk wanted to make a bigger difference than ever before. As banana peels were laid in front of his path, he tried to surf them. He screamed more loudly and more intense then ever. The nuts would fall, the squirrels and monkey would laugh.

Slip sliding away,
       Slip sliding away,
              CRASH! Chipmunk woke up next to the tree.

Chipmunk knew he was doing the best. He was making a difference
Raccoon was sneaking around placing nuts in various places.
Chipmunk now laughed and smiled, laying on his back on the ground,
admiring those monkeys, he once thought were so crazy.
Chipmunk realized he was a monkey too, and we are all a bit nutty. As another set of nuts flew into the air from his stuffed cheeks, Chipmunk glimpsed Raccoon climbing the tree. He had learned a lot about life from Raccoon, but he always could relate to being a monkey himself.

On the ground, laid another banana peel and Mr. Chipmunk dazed.

Oops!

Chipmunk stood up and took a bow.